TYRANNOSAURUS REX
REVISED EDITION

A TRUE BOOK®

by

Elaine Landau

Children's Press®
A Division of Scholastic Inc.

New York Toronto London Auckland Sydney
Mexico City New Delhi Hong Kong

The fierce
Tyrannosaurus rex

Content Consultant
Susan H. Gray, MS, Zoology,
Little Rock, Arkansas

Reading Consultant
Cecilia Minden-Cupp, PhD
*Former Director, Language and
Literacy Program
Harvard Graduate School of
Education*

Author's Dedication
For Hailey

*The photograph on the cover
and the title page shows a
model of Tyrannosaurus rex.*

Library of Congress Cataloging-in-Publication Data
Landau, Elaine.
   Tyrannosaurus rex / by Elaine Landau. — Rev. ed.
      p. cm. — (A true book)
   Includes bibliographical references and index.
   ISBN-10: 0-531-16832-8 (lib. bdg.)   0-531-15472-6 (pbk.)
   ISBN-13: 978-0-531-16832-5 (lib. bdg.)   978-0-531-15472-4 (pbk.)
   1. Tyrannosaurus rex—Juvenile literature. I. Title. II. Series.
QE862.S3L37 2007
567.912'9—dc22
                                                              2006004426

CHILDREN'S PRESS, and A TRUE BOOK™, and associated logos are
trademarks and/or registered trademarks of Scholastic Library Publishing.
SCHOLASTIC and associated logos are trademarks and/or registered
trademarks of Scholastic Inc.
1 2 3 4 5 6 7 8 9 10 R 16 15 14 13 12 11 10 09 08 07

Contents

Tyrannosaurus rex means "king of the tyrant lizards."

King of the Tyrant Lizards

Imagine a huge dinosaur standing in front of you. It is one of the largest meat eaters ever to walk the earth. It is ready to attack. As it charges, you see its curved, knifelike teeth. They line the dinosaur's powerful 4-foot (1.2-meter)-long jaws. You are about to be eaten by a frightening flesh eater. Its name is *Tyrannosaurus rex*, meaning "king of the **tyrant** lizards."

Luckily, there is no need to panic. You will never find yourself in this scary spot. *Tyrannosaurus rex*, along with the rest of the dinosaurs, no longer exists. But if you would like to know more about the King of the Tyrant Lizards, read on.

New Kid on the Block

*T*yrannosaurus rex lived about 68 million to 65 million years ago during the Age of the Dinosaurs. The Age of the Dinosaurs lasted from about 250 million years ago to about 65 million years ago. *Tyrannosaurus rex* was one of the last kinds of dinosaurs to roam Earth. It is called a theropod, or meat eater.

Tyrannosaurus rex was one of the fiercest hunters to live during the Age of Dinosaurs.

Seeing *Tyrannosaurus rex* up close must have been scary for many smaller dinosaurs.

Up Close with a Flesh-Eating Giant

Seeing *Tyrannosaurus rex* up close might have been pretty scary. This dinosaur weighed 14,000 pounds (6,350 kilograms), or about 7 tons. The largest *Tyrannosaurus rex* known was 42 feet (13 m)

long. That's as long as a really big school bus!

Tyrannosaurus rex measured about 13 feet (4 m) high at its hip. That is taller than one tall man standing on another tall man's shoulders.

Look at the tiny arms and two-fingered hands on this *Tyrannosaurus rex* skeleton. Scientists (like the one standing beside the skeleton) don't know exactly how the dinosaur used such small limbs.

Tyrannosaurus rex was even more impressive rearing up on its hind legs in a fight. Then it was 18 feet (5 m) high. That is as tall as a giraffe—the tallest animal in the world today!

Tyrannosaurus rex also had a large head. Its skull was 5 feet (1.5 m) long and weighed about 600 pounds (272 kg).

This dinosaur had good eyesight and hearing. *Tyrannosaurus rex* also had an excellent sense of smell. These senses would have been useful in finding **prey**. Prey is an animal that is hunted by other animals for food.

Perhaps *Tyrannosaurus rex* is best known for its large

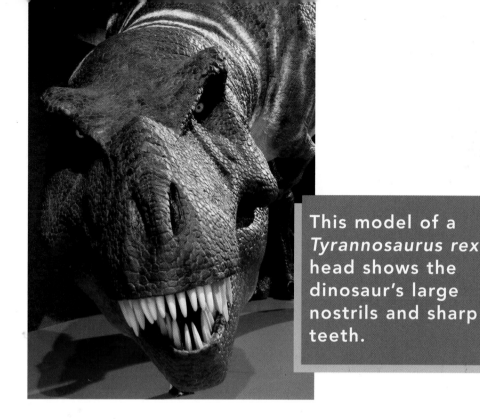

This model of a *Tyrannosaurus rex* head shows the dinosaur's large nostrils and sharp teeth.

mouth and scary teeth. This dinosaur's mouth was meant for eating huge chunks of meat from prey. Its lower jaw could tear off large mouthfuls of meat. Its teeth were strong enough to crush bones.

Tyrannosaurus rex had fifty-eight teeth. The teeth were as sharp as daggers and the size of bananas. Some were 12 inches (30 centimeters) long! *Tyrannosaurus rex*'s teeth have been compared to the blade of a steak knife. That is because its teeth had **serrated**, or jagged, edges. This allowed them to rip through flesh more easily.

Tyrannosaurus rex tore apart its meal by gripping the

prey with its teeth and swinging its head back and forth. It did not matter if some of its teeth fell out. The teeth always grew back.

The fossilized neck, head, and teeth of a *Tyrannosaurus rex*

Paleontologists—scientists who study **prehistoric** life— are not sure how many years *Tyrannosaurus rex* lived. Some think that this dinosaur might have reached the ripe old age of about one hundred years. After all, dinosaurs were **reptiles**. Some of today's large reptiles, such as the crocodile, can live for many years.

These dinosaurs probably died young, however. Some paleontologists believe that no

A paleontologist cleans the jaw-bone of a *Tyrannosaurus rex*.

Tyrannosaurus rex lived past age thirty. However, paleontologists are still arguing over how long *Tyrannosaurus rex* lived.

Tyrannosaurus rex was a meat eater, which means it ate other dinosaurs and reptiles.

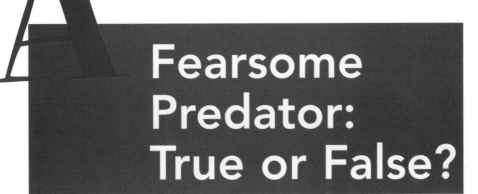

A Fearsome Predator: True or False?

Was *Tyrannosaurus rex* really a frightening **predator**? Predators are animals that hunt other animals for food. Did *Tyrannosaurus rex* kill its prey with speed and ease? Books and movies often show this dinosaur this way. Some paleontologists have been wondering if this idea is true.

   Tyrannosaurus rex may have been too large and bulky to catch its prey easily. Computer models have been developed to learn more about animal behavior. Some computer models show how much muscle an animal needs to be able to run. Things such as the animal's height, weight, and posture are considered.

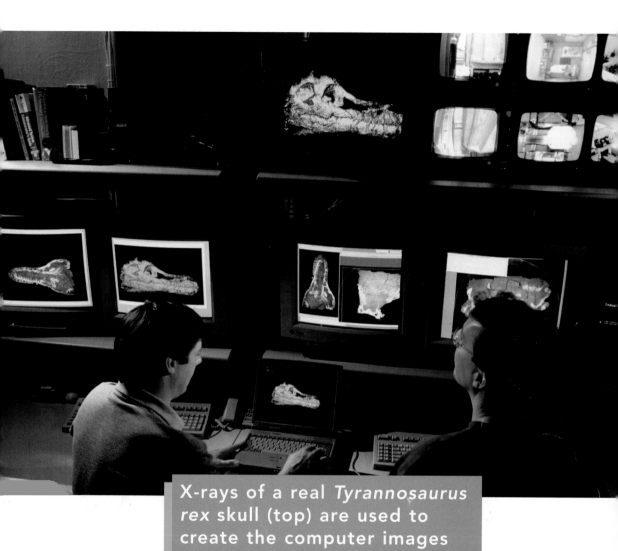

X-rays of a real *Tyrannosaurus rex* skull (top) are used to create the computer images on the screens (below).

These models have been useful in studying *Tyrannosaurus rex*. The models show that this dinosaur did not have enough leg muscle to move quickly.

Tyrannosaurus rex probably moved at a speed of no more than 15 miles (24 kilometers) per hour.

Fully grown, *Tyrannosaurus rex* probably walked at a speed of only about 6 miles (10 kilometers) an hour. Even at its fastest, *Tyrannosaurus rex* probably could not have reached more than 15 miles (24 km) an hour. Today's elephants can run twice as fast.

It is doubtful that *Tyrannosaurus rex* was ever a high-speed killing machine. Some plant-eating dinosaurs were not very fast on their feet, either. So *Tyrannosaurus rex* would have been fast enough to catch, kill, and eat them.

It is likely that *Tyrannosaurus rex* was also a scavenger. This means that it ate parts of dead dinosaurs that had been left to rot. Some paleontologists believe that *Tyrannosaurus rex* would scare off smaller, faster predators and steal the meals they left behind.

Tyrannosaurus rex sometimes ate the meat of dead dinosaurs.

Walks Like a Cat, with Legs and Feet Like a Bird

Paleontologists think that *Tyrannosaurus rex* probably walked bent over. This way, its large tail would not touch the ground. Paleontologists also think that *Tyrannosaurus rex* walked on its toes like a cat. Cats do not drag their tails along the ground either.

Tyrannosaurus rex's feet looked like those of a bird

Tyrannosaurus rex's hind, or rear, legs were quite large. They were about 12 to 13 feet (nearly 4 m) tall. Its feet were interesting, too. *Tyrannosaurus rex* had three toes on each foot. The toes looked a lot like the feet of today's birds—only much, much bigger!

The fossilized toe bone of a *Tyrannosaurus rex*

Tyrannosaurus rex had large, powerful hind legs.

Finding Fossils

Paleontologists learned about *Tyrannosaurus rex* through **fossils**. Fossils are evidence of plants and animals that lived long ago. Fossils might include bones, footprints, teeth, or leaf imprints on rocks. Paleontologists carefully dig up fossils and

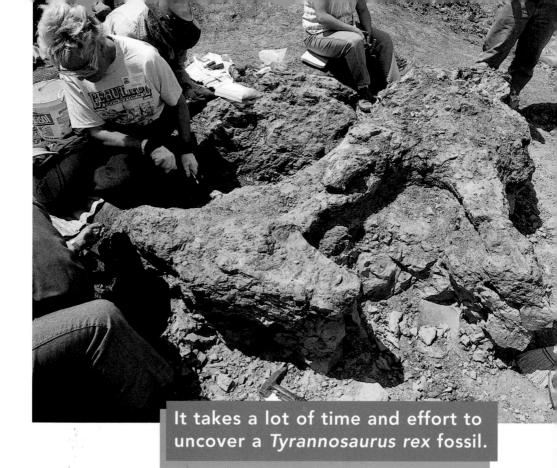

It takes a lot of time and effort to uncover a *Tyrannosaurus rex* fossil.

put them together like the
pieces of a jigsaw puzzle.
Then they see what the animals that existed on Earth in
prehistoric times looked like.

Tyrannosaurus rex lived in what are now Montana, Colorado, New Mexico, Wyoming, South Dakota, and southwestern Canada. The first nearly complete skeleton of this dinosaur was discovered in northern Montana in 1902. An American paleontologist named Henry Fairchild Osborn studied the fossils. In 1905, he gave the dinosaur its official name— *Tyrannosaurus rex*.

This map shows areas where *Tyranno-saurus rex* fossils have been found.

Other *Tyrannosaurus rex* fossils have been found. One of the most important discoveries occurred on August 12, 1990. Fossil hunter Sue Hendrickson was looking for dinosaur fossils near Faith,

Sue, on display at the Field Museum in Chicago, Illinois

South Dakota. While looking at some cliffs, she found huge dinosaur bones. She thought that they might be *Tyranno-saurus rex* bones—and she was right. Hendrickson had discovered one of the largest, most complete *Tyrannosaurus rex* skeletons ever found. Those on her team nicknamed the dinosaur Sue.

Sue the dinosaur's bones were in great condition. Paleontologists could even

A paleontologist prepares fossils for display to visitors.

see where muscles once attached to the bones. Paleontologists have already learned a lot about these dinosaurs from studying Sue's skeleton. Today, the skeleton is on display at The Field Museum of Natural History in Chicago, Illinois. People from all over the United States and other countries visit the museum for an up-close view of Sue.

The Dinosaur Disappearance

Many people think that all the dinosaurs died out at once. But that is not how it happened. Dinosaurs roamed the earth for about 180 million years. However, no single kind of dinosaur lasted for all that time. At different times

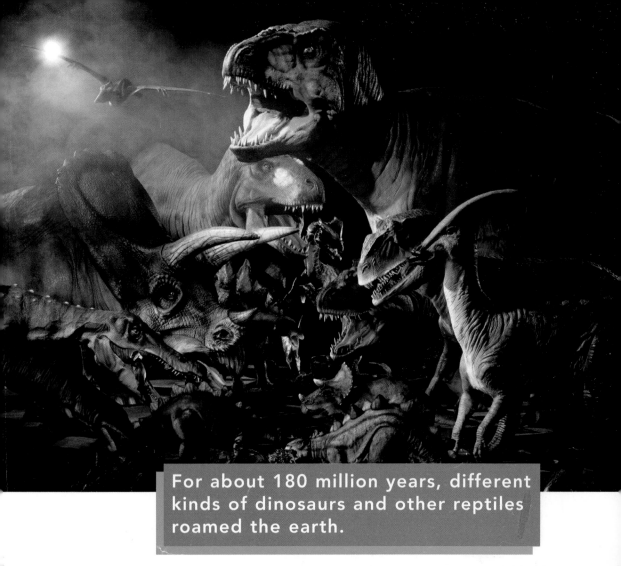

For about 180 million years, different kinds of dinosaurs and other reptiles roamed the earth.

during the Age of the Dinosaurs, different kinds of dinosaurs appeared and died out.

Near the end of the Age of the Dinosaurs, all the dinosaurs, including *Tyrannosaurus rex*, became extinct, or died out. This did not happen overnight. It took place slowly, over about a million years.

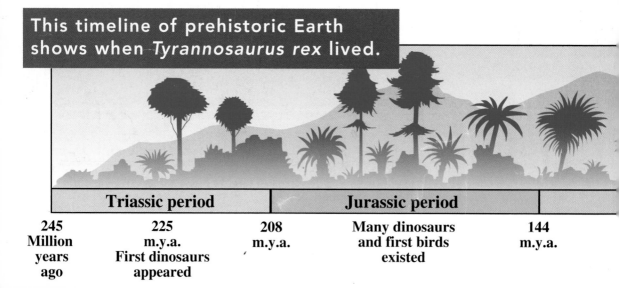

This timeline of prehistoric Earth shows when *Tyrannosaurus rex* lived.

Triassic period		Jurassic period	
245 Million years ago	225 m.y.a. First dinosaurs appeared	208 m.y.a.	Many dinosaurs and first birds existed	144 m.y.a.

No one knows for sure what caused the dinosaurs to become extinct. They may have died out after an asteroid crashed into Earth. Asteroids are large, planetlike bodies that move through space.

(Note: "m.y.a." means "million years ago")

| Cretaceous period | Tertiary period | |

68-65 m.y.a.
Tyrannosaurus rex
existed

65 m.y.a
Last dinosaurs
became extinct

1.6
m.y.a.
First humans
appeared

If an asteroid struck Earth, a huge crater, or hole, would have been created. The dust from the force of the asteroid hitting the ground would have floated up into the **atmosphere**. These dust particles would have formed thick, dark clouds that blocked out the sun. Without sunlight, the weather on Earth would have become quite cold. Paleontologists believe dinosaurs could not

Paleontologists believe the cold climate that followed an asteroid collision with Earth caused *Tyrannosaurus rex* and other dinosaurs to die out.

Museum displays of *Tyrannosaurus rex* skeletons will interest visitors for a long time to come.

have survived in such a **climate**.

During the Age of the Dinosaurs, Earth was still changing. The large landmasses called continents had not finished forming. Seas and mountain ranges were still taking shape. Different kinds of plant life appeared. The dinosaurs were unable to get used to all these changes and probably died out as a result.

Tyrannosaurus rex will never return. We can still learn about this fierce meat eater from museums and books. That's about as close as most of us would like to get anyway!

To Find Out More

Here are some additional resources to help you learn more about *Tyrannosaurus rex*:

 **Books**

Dalla Vecchia, Fabio Marco. **Tyrannosaurus rex**. Blackbirch, 2004.

Gray, Susan H. **Tyrannosaurus rex**. Child's World, 2004.

Holtz, Thomas R. **T. Rex: Hunter or Scavenger?** Random House, 2003.

Schomp, Virginia. **Tyrannosaurus**. Benchmark, 2003.

Skrepnick, Michael. **Tyrannosaurus Rex: Fierce King of the Dinosaurs**. Enslow, 2005.

Organizations and Online Sites

Prehistoric Life—
Tyrannosaurus rex
http://www.museum.vic.gov. au/prehistoric/dinosaurs/ trex.html

Visit this Web site to learn about *Tyrannosaurus rex* and its relatives.

Project Exploration
950 East 61st Street
Chicago, IL 60637
http://www.info@projectex- ploration.org/

This organization works to increase students' interest in paleontology.

Sue at the Field Museum
http://www.fieldmuseum.org/ sue/

Learn all about one of the largest *Tyrannosaurus rex* ever discovered.

Important Words

atmosphere the blanket of gases that
surrounds Earth

climate the usual weather in a place

fossils evidence of plants and animals that
lived long ago. Fossils might include bones,
footprints, teeth, or leaf imprints on rocks.

predator an animal that hunts other animals
for food

prehistoric from the time before history
was recorded

prey an animal that is hunted by another
animal for food

reptiles cold-blooded animals that crawl on
the ground or creep on short legs

serrated having a jagged edge

tyrant someone who rules other people in
a cruel or unjust way

Index

Meet the Author

A ward-winning author Elaine Landau worked as a newspaper reporter, an editor, and a youth-services librarian before becoming a full-time writer. She has written more than 250 nonfiction books for young people, including True Books on animals, countries, and food. Ms. Landau has a bachelor's degree in English and journalism from New York University as well as a master's degree in library and information science. She lives with her husband and son in Miami, Florida.